CLOSING SALES
AND
WINNING THE
CUSTOMER'S HEART

CLOSING SALES AND WINNING THE CUSTOMER'S HEART

by
Emily King Parker

CRISP PUBLICATIONS

Closing Sales and Winning the Customer's Heart
Emily King Parker

CREDITS:
Editor: George Young
Book and Cover Design and Production: Fifth Street Design, Berkeley, CA

Printed in the United States of America by Von Hoffmann Graphics

http:/www.crisplearning.com

Crisp Publications, Inc. Menlo Park, CA 94025

Distribution to the U.S. Trade:
National Book Network, Inc.
4720 Boston Way
Lanham, MD 20706
1-800-462-6420

99 00 01 02 03   10 9 8 7 6 5 4 3 2 1

Library of Congress Card Number 99-75057
King Parker, Emily
ISBN 1-56052-565-7

Contents

Creating Sales

Motivate! Motivate! Motivate! Motivation has long been thought to hold the key to more sales. Sales managers have put their minds to creating dynamic sales incentives and commission structures, in the hopes of motivating their sales teams to produce more.

Motivation is not a bad thing. But it isn't the only thing, and other things should come before motivational training and incentives. After all, motivation does not **create** success in sales, it supports it. **Skills create success in sales**.

No incentive, no matter how appealing it is, and no commission structure, no matter how generous it is, can make people do what they are **unable** to do.

Even an incentive plan promising fifty cents on every dollar could only yield limited results. Beyond the limits of ability, additional incentives can only generate frustration. Incentives cannot enable people to sell **beyond** their ability. Only new skills can do that.

The skills I am referring to are not the usual sales techniques of opening and closing sales, overcoming objections and price negotiation. Those techniques should be your foundation - they should be solid if you want to go anywhere in sales. And they can be learned in training programs or in numerous books on the market about basic sales.

What I am referring to are **superior interpersonal skills**. Superior interpersonal skills strengthen your basic techniques and catapult you into a higher league of sales. Many people who sell for a living think they already possess these skills. After reading this book, they may see things a little differently.

After reading this book and considering the **Success Builder** exercises (through discussion or written response), **you** — a sales pro like me — will see that more is possible, and that you can gain new skills to help you generate more sales, have more fun, and motivate yourself.

Skills come first and lead to sales success, which in itself is motivating. Sales success creates its own motivation for more sales success.

So keep reading. You are about to become a superior seller.

Breaking Bad Habits

Learning to communicate and cooperate effectively with customers is the single most valuable skill a sales professional can have. The easiest way to attain this skill is to constantly stretch your own point of view to include other perspectives.

A common mistake made by us sales pros is expecting everyone — every client or potential client — to be just like us. We tend to communicate from our own point of view. If we take a moment to think about it, logic tells us this expectation is unrealistic. The chances of clients being just like us are a lot slimmer than the chances of them being different from us, and in important ways that impact how well we will communicate with them.

Let me give an example. You're familiar with the dilemma of the glass: is it half full or half empty? Let's pretend I'm the kind of person who sees the glass as half full, and I'm trying to sell it to someone who sees it as half empty. I'm selling it as a half-full glass, because that is what I value about it. But it's not what the customer values.

The customer values that, because it is half empty, it will be less likely to spill as it is carried out of the room. But I'm not thinking about that because it's obvious to me that the clear benefit of the glass is that it's half full. If I can't broaden my view of this glass — and fast — I'm going to lose the sale.

Here's another example. Would you agree that some people tend to see things literally and others see things figuratively? In other words, one person would look at a fork and say, "this is a fork, it will always be a fork and nothing else." Someone else might say, "yes, it is a fork, but it can be used as an antenna and — oh yeah! — I used to have a bracelet made out of a fork! A fork can be a lot of things, not just an eating device."

There is ample room for misunderstanding and negative judgement here! These two look at the fork, look at each other and roll their eyes. The first says, "Listen space cadet, stop reading so much into the fork already!" The second responds with, "At least I have some imagination - all you see is what's right in front of you. How boring!"

We can't afford this kind of misunderstanding and negative judgement if we want success in sales. Understanding different personality styles will help us present our product so that it appeals to everyone — not just us. It will also help us to prevent costly breakdowns in communication.

Another common mistake in sales is to flaunt our product knowledge so that it intimidates clients and prospects. For example, those of us selling high-tech products and services need to be aware of the fact that our customers do not always have the level of expertise we do. That is why they come to us, as sales professionals. Not only do we write the sale, but we are presumed to have knowledge of the product we are selling.

If we intimidate customers with jargon, fail to explain complex ideas, fail to explain simple ideas if necessary, and cause them to feel like idiots, we will end up feeling smart, and they will end up taking their business elsewhere. This is no way to treat a prospective customer.

The ability to breakdown a concept or process into its smallest parts so that non-experts can understand them is a valuable skill. The ability to create logic for someone, to explain how and why things are done as they are, is critical to selling anything.

It may be assumed that because you know all there is to know about your product, you can sell it. Bad assumption. If you are in sales, it doesn't matter that you have more technical expertise than anyone you know. If you can't close sales and build repeat clientele, you won't be in sales very long!

There is no substitute for good sales technique and the ability to interact effectively with prospects. Of course, every sales-person thinks they have this ability. But it is extremely difficult to see ourselves objectively. We all have blind spots — aspects of ourselves we simply do not see. We, ourselves, erect barriers which we can easily spot in others but fail to see in ourselves.

I have a list of four rules — I call them "never-nevers" — about working with customers. And, because you want to sell more, and I want you to sell more, I will share them with you.

THE NEVER-NEVERS

1. Never make people feel inferior
2. Never try to impress with jargon
3. Never take existing customers for granted
4. Never compete with the customer

Being an expert at whatever it is you are selling does not necessarily mean you are good at selling it, nor does it mean that you are better at selling it than someone with less expertise. Most important, being an expert does not give you license to make people — customers — feel like idiots. This covers the first two never-nevers.

Rule number three tells us never to take for granted our existing customers. This is as important as the first two rules. Nothing is a sure thing in sales, but if there were an **almost** — sure thing, it would be your base of existing clients. They are more likely to buy than cold prospects are. In fact, in many cases your time is more wisely spent cultivating repeat business than massaging cold leads.

Never compete with customers. The only thing you'll win is the satisfaction of "out-doing" a customer. You'll lose the sale and the sales of all the people this person will tell about you. If customers challenge you, it's for one of these reasons:

1. They need accurate information and feel you are unable to provide it. This is legitimate and shame on you if you are dol-ing out wrong-isms or withholding information to close sales.

2. They need to feel smart themselves. If you make them feel stupid when they are trying to show you they are smart, you lose. They will buy from someone who appreciates and acknowledges their smarts. Your chances of closing this person are better if you make them feel as smart as they want you to think they are.

These never-nevers sound pretty obvious, don't they?

So ask yourself, "Am I in sales to show how smart I am, or am I in sales to make money?"

If you answer that you are in sales to show how smart you are, stop reading and give this book to someone who's not as smart. If you answered that you are in sales to make money, then read on because the journey to success is about to begin.

Personality Styles: Introduction

As human beings, we share some unusual habits. For example, we tend to misjudge each other. With little or no information, we come to judgments — positive and negative — that are often wrong. We may find that we've missed out on a great friendship or professional opportunity. Or, we may be unpleasantly surprised when a person we have positively prejudged disappoints us. After all, what are prejudgments but our own expectations, based on past experience, that we project onto others?

Without really giving people a chance, we make important decisions about their desirability based on very little information. On the basis of something as limited as a brief conversation, we make our decision. We decide they are different from us and, what's more, different in a way that makes them undesirable. Then we either tune them out, become offensive or defensive, and bring the interaction to a close. We do this because we have biases.

Let me give an example of bias.

Diane is the director of a retail art gallery. One day a woman entered the gallery and began looking around. She was somewhat unkempt looking, with tousled hair, old jeans and a t-shirt. She even wore cowboy boots. Not the usual patron of Diane's shop. Nonetheless, Diane noticed with displeasure that none of her staff were approaching the woman. They had obviously made the same observations about her appearance that Diane had, and decided that this woman was just another "looker" with no money to spend. No one to take seriously.

Diane approached the woman herself and engaged her in conversation. As it turned out, the woman was on vacation from a sprawling ranch in Wyoming, where she happened to own an impressive collection of original western art.

The unkempt looking woman made a sizable purchase with Diane before leaving that day; a purchase any sales professional would take seriously.

Judging a book by its cover is something we all do. If it weren't, the expression would never have been coined. I don't presume to know if it's something we do by nature or because of the way we are socialized. But I do know that it's something we can choose to keep in check. As sales professionals it is something we **must** choose to keep in check.

Bias is the enemy of anyone in sales. As professional sellers we, perhaps more than any other group, are called upon to interact and build relationships with people from all over the world. We cannot afford to hide behind stereotypes and negative characterizations of people who are different from us. We are challenged with facing and overcoming our biases and doing it fairly quickly. The world is indeed shrinking and we are interacting with cultures from every part of the globe.

The story of the unexpected art collector is but one example of how sales professionals do themselves in with bias — and of how they can benefit from overcoming those biases as Diane did. But what about overcoming biases against people with different values, perceptions, and personality styles? After all, it is easy to deal with our assumptions about a person's taste in clothes and physical appearance. We simply tell ourselves, "don't judge a book by its cover." But in order to become truly effective with customers of all kinds, we need more than cliches - we need new skills.

New skills and information are what we need to form a new and better attitude about customers and sales. This book combines sales and psychology in a way no book has before. The end result will mean more sales for you, and more fun working with customers.

Success Builder

1. What are some of your biases?

2. What awareness did you gain about yourself from this chapter?

3. What awareness did you gain about others?

Personality Styles: Basic Training

Over 60 years ago, a Swiss psychologist by the name of Carl G. Jung (pronounced "Young") observed that certain human behaviors seemed so predictable, they might arise from natural preference. Jung did not attribute these preferences to any particular environment. Rather, he perceived them to be an innate part of humans — the part that defines our unique personalities.

Later, in the 1930's, a mother-daughter team by the name of Katherine Briggs and Isabel Briggs Myers put Jung's theory to work, developing a classification system which is now called the Myers-Briggs Type Indicator® (MBTI®) instrument. The MBTI is similar to a multiple choice questionnaire and sorts responses into one of sixteen personality "Type" categories. This instrument is a powerfully accurate tool for self- understanding and for understanding others.

We each have eight elements to our personality type, but of those eight, we naturally prefer four of them. That means we are more comfortable or familiar with some elements than with others, even though they all exist within us. An example I often use to illustrate this concept in training classes is catching a ball. If I called to you before tossing a ball, you could probably catch it with either hand. But if I simply tossed the ball with no warning you would instinctively reach out with your dominant hand. The elements of a personality type include the following preferences.

Myers-Briggs Type Indicator and (MBTI) are the registered trademarks of Consulting Psychologists Press, Inc.

I am including descriptive adjectives commonly used to characterize each preference. Keep in mind these descriptions are based on generalizations and should be used as guidelines, not gospel.

Extraversion or Introversion

* talkative	* reflective
* responsive	* reserved
* accessible	* private
* broad interests	* deep interests
* encompassing	* focusing

Extraversion (**E**) and Introversion (**I**) are related to whether we are energized by the external world of people and things (**E**), or the internal world of thoughts and ideas (**I**). They don't relate to whether or not we enjoy people and things, simply in what amounts.

Gather Info

Sensing or Intuition

* realistic	* imaginative
* here & now	* future-oriented
* sees things literally	* sees meaning in things
* concrete perspective	* abstract perspective
* specifics, facts	* generalities, ideas

Sensing (**S**) and iNtuition (**N**) are related to how we perceive the world around us. Are we inclined to see things as they are (**S**) or as they could be (**N**)?

Making Decisions

Thinking or Feeling

* objective	* subjective
* tough-minded	* warm-hearted
* prioritize fairness	* prioritize kindness
* critical analysis	* promote harmony
* non-personal	* personal

11

Thinking (**T**) and Feeling (**F**) are related to how we go about making decisions about what we see in the world. Of course we all think and we all feel, but when it comes to making a decision or analyzing a situation, do we approach it objectively (**T**), focusing on the facts involved or do we approach it subjectively (**F**), focusing on the people and our own subjective values.

Lifestyle + what we show the world!

Judging or Perceiving

* structured	* spontaneous
* decisive	* flexible
* seeks closure	* open-ended
* lists & schedules	* impulse & options
* planful	* playful

Judging (**J**) and Perceiving (**P**) relate to our life-styles and the face we show the world. In other words, once we have gathered information (**S/N**) and made decisions about it (**T/F**), what do we show the world; Judging or Perceiving? When you look at your four choices together — one from each line — you are looking at your personality type.

These are the 16 possible types:

ISTJ ISFJ INFJ INTJ ISTP ISFP INFP INTP

ESTP ESFP ENFP ENTP ESTJ ESFJ ENFJ ENTJ

Understanding personality types is a great inoculation against bias. Each of the sixteen types is equally valid, and each has pros and cons. But no one type is better or worse than any other. Just different, each type has strengths and weaknesses. Looking at the world from this point of view helps us to lay aside our prejudices against people whose skin, language, culture, gender, age, abilities or lifestyle are different from ours.

Once we agree to look at one another from this perspective, we will have more tolerance for those people who test our patience. We will realize, instead, that their intention is not necessarily to ruffle our feathers. They simply view and act upon the world differently than we do and, as this book suggests, have a lot to contribute towards a balanced view of things. As sales professionals, we must have a balanced view of those we serve because they come to us in all personality types and varieties within those types.

Self-awareness and awareness of differing personalty styles is a powerful combination when it comes to interacting with a prospective customer or client. The more we know of our clients and their styles, the better able we will be to give good service. The first step toward improvement is *recognizing a need for improvement*. Only then can we overcome our blind spots and build on our strengths.

Success Builder:

1. Which of the adjectives on the previous pages describe you best?

2. Which describe you least?

3. Which adjectives describe your "typical" customer?

4. What awareness did you gain about yourself and others in this chapter?

Personality Styles
and Selling

Given all this new information, you may be asking, "But how can it help me improve my sales?" That is a good question. The answer is what makes this book different from others on the subject of personality types. For now, suffice it to say that if the personality preferences discussed in the last chapter apply to us and help us understand ourselves better, they can also help us understand our customers.

Let us take this moment to debunk the unspoken assumption that all customers are alike, the only difference being whether or not they have the good sense to buy from us. Customers are people and people have different personalities. As discussed earlier, peoples' personalities have different elements and we must understand them in order to communicate effectively.

Let me propose that the eight preferences described in chapter four correspond to the four stages of a sale. They are listed as follows, first from the seller's point of view, then from the customer's point of view.

SELLER'S POINT OF VIEW

APPROACH   Relating to the customer
OBSERVE   Presenting the product as you see it
ASSESS   Guiding the decision process
ACT   Closing the sale & following up

CUSTOMER'S POINT OF VIEW

APPROACH   Relating to you, the seller

OBSERVE   Looking at the product

ASSESS   Deciding whether or not to buy

ACT   Making the purchase

Can you see where the personality preferences fit into this process? Let's clarify it this way:

APPROACH   You relate to customers in an Extraverted or Introverted way and they to you.

OBSERVE   You see the product from a Sensing or iNtuitive lens and customers see it from their preferred lenses.

ASSESS   You guide the decision from a Thinking or Feeling stance, and customers make the decision according to their preferences for Thinking or Feeling.

ACT   You close the sale in a Judging or Perceiving manner and the customer makes the purchase in a Judging or Perceiving manner.

To test your initial understanding of these ideas, take a few minutes to think about the way you approach, observe, assess, and act. Circle your choice for each stage of the sale below:

APPROACH

Extraversion or Introversion

OBSERVE

Sensing or iNtuition

ASSESS

Thinking or Feeling

ACT

Judging or Perceiving

Now give the other choices — the four you did not choose for yourself — to an imaginary customer. Better yet, think of a client or customer you have interacted with more than a few times. Guess at their preferences and circle the letters below:

APPROACH

Extraversion or Introversion

OBSERVE

Sensing or iNtuition

ASSESS

Thinking or Feeling

ACT

Judging or Perceiving

Now look at the differences between your choices for yourself and for the customer. Do you think you approach things similarly? Observe things similarly? Assess and Act on the sale similarly? If so, what can you learn about working effectively with that person? If not — if there are differences — what can be learned from them?

Let's say you prefer an Introverted approach style. Your approach to the customer, either in the form of a cold call or a qualified lead, may be described in these terms: low-key, saying only what's necessary, listening more than talking. If the customer, on the other hand, has an Extraverted approach, you may find yourself losing control of the sales situation because they talk more, talk louder, and more forcefully.

The reverse of this is equally challenging. You, the seller, have an Extraverted style of approach to the customer, which might look something like this: enthused, talking more than listening, giving too much information. The customer, with an Introverted style of approach to you, might seem to be unresponsive or uninterested. S/he might seem aloof or skeptical. S/he might not give you many verbal or visual clues as to how s/he feels about what you are selling.

Now imagine you both share the same style of approach. If you both have an Introverted approach, there is the danger of too little needed information being shared, either because the customer doesn't ask or you don't volunteer — or both. If, on the other hand, you both have Extraverted styles of approach, you might run the risk of talking over each other, interrupting each other, and missing important steps in the selling/buying process.

The exercise above is one you should become familiar with. Do it again when you have finished reading this book — perhaps your responses will change. The goal is for you to make these ideas part of your approach to every customer and prospect. With practice, you will begin to think about preferences naturally and automatically, and your sales effectiveness will improve by leaps and bounds.

The next two charts match up typological preferences (E, I, S, N, T, F, J, P) with stages of a sale (approach, observe, assess, act), and provide easy-to-remember descriptive phrases. The first chart is from the point of view of the salesperson, the second from the point of view of the customer. As always, these are general guidelines, not hard and fast rules. Remember, individuals are more complex than just four preferences. Take care not to presume too much about a customer with too little information.

APPROACH-OBSERVE-ASSESS-ACT
(SELLER)

APPROACH	E: friendly, talkative, enthused
	I: reserved, listens, allows silence
OBSERVE	S: attentive to details, gives specific and practical answers to questions
	N: shares interesting aspects of product, gives general answers to questions
ASSESS	T: closing style emphasizes logical, unsentimental rationale (e.g., investment value to customer)
	F: closing style emphasizes sentiment, personal appeal (e.g., good feeling for customer)
ACT	J: closing is made in a clear, direct fashion; conscientiously follows up with clients for future sales and good will
	P: closing is made in a softer, more tentative manner; follow-up with clients may be sporadic, if at all

APPROACH-OBSERVE-ASSESS-ACT
(CUSTOMER)

APPROACH	E: friendly, talkative, responsive
	I: reserved, distant, less responsive
OBSERVE	S: attentive to details, wants clear answers to questions, practical
	N :bored by details, asks general questions about interesting aspects of product
ASSESS	T: decision to buy may be based on logic, facts, without sentiment
	F: decision to buy may be based on impulse, instinct, sentiment, likes and dislikes
ACT	J: actual purchase may be made in a decisive manner, with out "hemming & hawing"
	P: actual purchase may be put off until last minute, after options have been explored

Before we go any further, it is important to consider a word of caution. Using concepts of personality types can be valuable to you in sales, tremendously valuable. I would not have written this book if I did not truly believe this.

Using the information to try to manipulate or control customers is not what this book is about.

My first experience with personality types happened to be in a sales context. I was applying for a job selling memberships to a dating service. The interviewer told me that one of the tactics they used in closing sales was to determine the "weak spot" in each potential member, based on their personality type. I found this distasteful and declined their job offer.

The use of information about individual styles to manipulate or persuade potential buyers is unethical. This book is not a guide to the "weak spot". Rather, this approach will guide you to a better understanding of yourself and your relationship to your product or service, as well as to your customer. It will illuminate your strengths and weaknesses, your likes and dislikes, and help you to evaluate your job satisfaction and success. All this will help you be more effective in sales.

BENEFITS OF EACH PREFERENCE IN SALES

E
- Focuses energy outward, engages the client
- Easily establishes rapport via light banter/shmoozing
- Seeks potential customers on and off the job

I
- Good at listening
- Able to summarize customer's needs
- Articulates in a few, well-chosen phrases

S
- Often masters details of the product/thorough knowledge
- Provides specific, clear answers to questions
- Realistic view of things

N
- Good at generating options and seeing possibilities
- Able to put purchase in larger perspective
- Able to communicate enthusiasm for the product

T
- Comfortable with the bottom-line dollars and cents element of sales
- Orients client to objective, logical reasons to buy
- Values quality

F
- Good at cultivating loyal customers
- Good at adding a personal touch to the buying experience
- Values what's best for customer

J
- Good at follow-up & tracking sales
- Organized
- Good at keeping focus & reaching closure

P
- Comfortable dealing with unpredictable events
- Able to give customer flexibility in decision-making process
- Able to guide the customer to "Yes" through exploratory questioning

LIABILITIES OF EACH PREFERENCE IN SALES

E • May talk too much, filling silences
  • May overwhelm buyer with too much information
  • May be redundant in the sales presentation, especially with a non-responsive introvert

I • May be too quiet and provide too little information
  • May internalize the interaction rather than fully participating with client
  • May not communicate energy for product being sold

S • May not readily generate options or be creative about selling
  • May not readily anticipate client needs, or future needs for product
  • May focus too much on detail, losing sight of the customer's needs

N • May generate too many options and lose sight of the client's focus
  • May disdain details and technical aspects of the product
  • May exaggerate or misrepresent product inadvertently, due to level of enthusiasm

T • May undervalue the emotional appeal of a product, focusing on the "bottom line"
  • May appear disinterested or arrogant
  • May value being right over making the sale

F • May avoid conflict over price (haggling)
  • May take lost sales personally
  • May not be bottom-line oriented enough to generate profits

J • May be too oriented to closing the sale, and appear pushy
  • May be impatient with slow decision-makers
  • May be inclined to tell customers what to do and why

P • May not be closure-oriented enough to complete sales
  • May not be thorough in follow-up efforts
  • May not see the need for timeliness

*For descriptions of each type of seller, see chapter twelve.

Success Builder

1. How do you most often Approach, Observe, Assess and Act in a sales situation?

2. How do you respond to customers who Approach, Observe, Assess and Act differently?

3. What awareness did you gain about yourself and others from this chapter?

Personality Styles and Buying

Understanding our own strengths and weaknesses is but half the picture when it comes to type. The other half of the picture — just as important as the first — is understanding others. After all, if we seek only to know ourselves, we may become self-righteous and intolerant. If we seek to know others as well, we will become receptive to their unique contributions.

As sales pros, understanding ourselves and others will help us work effectively with the wide variety of customers we encounter. Most people approach sales with the unconscious assumption that all customers and prospects are the same. They just wear different clothes, that's all. So we interact with them in one way — our way. If we make a connection, great! But the odds are against us. At best the odds are fifteen to one against us, because there are sixteen different personality types out there.

From this perspective, the next logical step is to explore the ways in which type is manifested in our customers. You will recognize some things, and some things will be new to you. My advice is to read with an open mind, and try to imagine your own customers as you consider the possibilities. One of the beauties of this approach to sales is that you can lay down this book and immediately put the concepts to work. Your next sales opportunity is also your next learning opportunity.

CLIENT TYPE

If the client:

is approachable and conversational

keeps the conversation going when there are lulls

shares personal information not directly related to the business at hand

talks through the decision-making process

He or she may be an Extravert

If the client:

looks quietly rather than approaching you

speaks relatively little, letting you do most of the talking

appears to think to him- or herself about the purchase

does not readily catch the contagion of your passion for the product

He or she may be an Introvert

If the client:

asks for specific information

emphasizes the practical aspects of the product

takes the things you say quite literally

shops for something to be used in the near future

He or she may be a Sensor

If the client:

asks general questions

appears to "tune out" when you get into the details of the product

does not focus on one thing for too long, before becoming interested in something else

is most intrigued by what is interesting about the product

He or she may be an iNtuitive

If the client:

appears skeptical at first, not easily won-over by your charm

is oriented to the bottom line, not necessarily to establishing rapport with you

asks you for information more than for opinions

bases the decision to buy or not buy on logical analysis of the costs and benefits

He or she may be a Thinker

If the client:

wants to interact with you in a friendly way

is interested in your opinions about the product

seems embarrassed about asking for a lower price

bases the decision to buy or not to buy on their "gut" feeling or other subjective means. e.g., what they like, what appeals

He or she may be a Feeler

If the client:

is straight-forward about what they like and dislike

shops with a purpose, and in advance

asks deliberate questions which they may read from a list they have brought with them

has little or no trouble making the decision to buy or not buy

He or she may be a Judger

If the client:

seems to enjoy browsing, with no particular focus

shops at the last minute

is open to suggestions

has difficulty deciding whether or not to buy, and what

He or she may be a Perceiver

As in all areas of personal and professional life, knowledge of the eight personality preferences and sixteen types is invaluable to us in sales. First, it helps reveal our own areas of effectiveness and ineffectiveness and, second, it allows us to be more attuned to the needs and style of each customer we encounter. Combined, this knowledge will improve the quality of our interactions with customers, and make the buying experience a pleasant one for all involved.

* For descriptions of each of the sixteen types of customers, see chapter thirteen.

Success Builder

1. Do you communicate more effectively with some styles than others? Explain.

2. How do you respond to customers who Approach, Observe, Assess and Act differently?

3. What awareness did you gain about yourself and others from this chapter?

Temperament Styles: Introduction

What often happens when people learn about personality types is that they become intensely interested in their own four preferences, and forget the rest. Of course they do. One cannot expect total recall from people who have merely read a book or attended a seminar. After all, there are 16 different types, and that's a lot of information.

But it is important to find some way to benefit from the information as it pertains to others. Remember the rule: understanding others is of equal importance to understanding ourselves, if we are to benefit from this information and improve sales.

A team by the name of David Keirsey and Marilyn Bates developed a way of seeing a snapshot of a person by looking at just two of their preferences. Keirsey and Bates refer to these two letters as the "Temperament." Temperaments are thought to be excellent predictors of behavior and personality in and of themselves, and a lot simpler to work with than 16 types! There are four temperaments, and no matter what your personality type is, one of the four temperaments belongs to you. First let me tell you what those special letter pairs are, then I'll explain how to figure out yours.

TEMPERAMENTS

iNtuitive & Feeling (NF)
iNtuitive & Thinking (NT)
Sensing & Judging (SJ)
Sensing & Perceiving (SP)

The chart on the following page shows the personality types that can be grouped with each of the four temperaments. They are shown as branches of a tree in order to demonstrate the connection between type and temperament. It is important to respect that personalities are made up of much more than just four preferences. Just as there are no two maple trees exactly alike, there are no two ENTJs exactly alike. The type and temperament simply help us understand each other better through identification of similarities. This is helpful because, as humans, we tend to respond more openly to things and people that are familiar to us than we do to things that are new and unknown.

The chart also contains adjectives that are commonly used in the discussion of temperaments. For more on temperaments, read "Please Understand Me," by Keirsey and Bates.

This observation is nothing new to sales professionals who find it easier to close sales to previous customers than with cold prospects. Repeat buyers have already put their faith in you once, and regard you — consciously or unconsciously — as a known factor. This allows you both to relax and proceed with meeting each others' needs. Following are examples of how you might recognize the four temperaments in a sales situation. After all, in real life, customers will not be approaching you with a hand outstretched and a pamphlet about their personality type and temperament. Instead, you will have to work with information gathered from your observations about them. Accompanying each example is an explanation of how it portrays temperament. These examples were collected from real people who sell for a living. Perhaps you will recognize yourself in some of them.

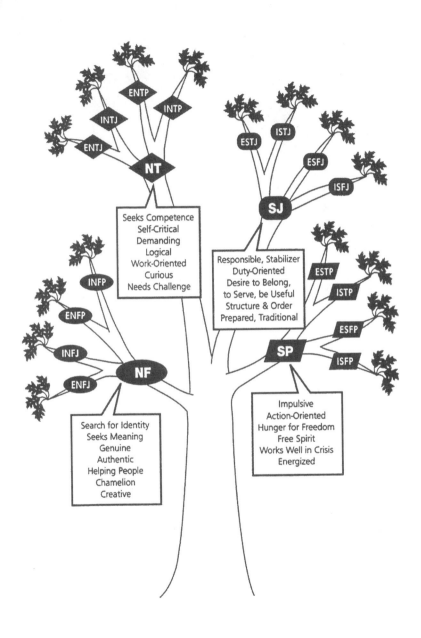

NT

Seeks Competence
Self-Critical
Demanding
Logical
Work-Oriented
Curious
Needs Challenge

SJ

Responsible, Stabilizer
Duty-Oriented
Desire to Belong,
to Serve, be Useful
Structure & Order
Prepared, Traditional

NF

Search for Identity
Seeks Meaning
Genuine
Authentic
Helping People
Chamelion
Creative

SP

Impulsive
Action-Oriented
Hunger for Freedom
Free Spirit
Works Well in Crisis
Energized

ENTP
INTP
INTJ
ENTJ
ESTJ
ISTJ
ESFJ
ISFJ
INFP
ENFP
INFJ
ENFJ
ESTP
ISTP
ESFP
ISFP

Success Builder

1. Which temperament style best describes you?

2. How do you see the four temperament styles in your world of customers and coworkers?

3. What awareness did you gain about yourself and others from this chapter?

Communication Gaps

To maintain a practical approach to the ideas presented in this book, I have opted not to give a lengthy explanation of temperament theory. Rather, let's understand it in real terms. The next section is made up of sample dialogue which clearly illustrate the concepts.

The following are examples of questions you may be asked by clients/customers with different temperament styles. The distinctions are subtle, and are included to heighten awareness of how misunderstandings can occur in interactions. As you read the examples, follow the words typed in **bold** for clues.

SJ "**Exactly** how much does this product/service cost?"

NT "What's the price **range** for this product/service?"

NF "How much are **you asking** for this product/service?"

SP "What do I have to **do** to get this?"

SJ "Tell me about the features of this product, as well as **how it is to be used**. When will **I have** to bring it in for service?"

NT "What's the **idea** behind this? I don't **understand** how it is supposed to work. How is it different from this other one?"

NF "I'd like to know **your opinion** of this one compared to the others you've demonstrated for us. Which do **you recommend?**"

SP "Can I see how it works?"

Take a moment — and a pen and pad — and jot down your initial observations about how these questions are different. In each case, what is being requested? What is it the customer needs from the salesperson? Based on your thoughts, take a stab at responding to each question to satisfy the customer.

Now we'll look at some practical suggestions for responding to these queries. There are more effective and less effective answers to each of them. The clues lie within the bold faced words. By learning the meanings underlying each of these questions, we will also discover what information the customer wants and understands, as opposed to phrasing things the way we might want them phrased for us.

SJ

Question: "Exactly how much does this cost?"

What Not To Say: "It's in the $8-10,000 **range**" or "Well, what would you consider a fair price?"

Because They Might Say/Think: "I asked for the price, and you're being evasive. I don't trust that." Or, they might become frustrated, thinking you don't understand what they're asking (and, in fact, you don't). A response like this just might insult or irritate the customer.

But You Might Try Saying This: "The price is $9,200 not including 5% sales tax, which brings the total to **exactly** $9,660 You'll only be asked to leave a 10% deposit, which is $920 — under $1,000!"

And They May Be More Likely To Say: "That sounds like a fair price. I'll take it."

Because: You have given them exactly what they asked for: the **exact** price.

❤ ❤ ❤ ❤ ❤ ❤ ❤ ❤

Question: "Tell me the features of this model, as well as how it is to be used and when I will have to bring it in for service?"

What Not To Say: "It will do whatever you want it to do!"

Because They Might Say/Think: "What in the world does **that** mean? You still haven't told me what it does and how. You aren't answering my question — are you being evasive?"

But You Might Try Saying: "I'll be glad to tell you about it! Let me take it step by step. First, you insert this piece into 'Area A'. Then, you'll notice the top pulls over like so. After that, lift it on the end that says "bottom" and flip the power switch. Now you're ready to go! By the way, there are excellent **instructions** for use, as well as **service**, which will tell you **exactly** how to **preserve** this piece of equipment for long-term use."

And They May Be More Likely To Say: "The parts are sturdy and well made. It seems clear enough how to assemble it...I'll take it."

NT

Question: "What's the price range for this?"

Don't Say: "The price is $9,200, not including 5% sales tax which brings it to $9,660."

Because they might say: "Aren't you willing to negotiate? What if I pay cash? No? I'll just go somewhere else."

But if you say: "The price is in the $8-10,000 **range**, which I am sure you have already guessed, given your **understanding** of the product."

They may well say: "Yes, I know a good price when I see one. I'll take it."

Because: You have shown them that you know they are **competent** and **knowledgeable** about the item. You have reinforced their image of themselves as the **expert**.

❤ ❤ ❤ ❤ ❤ ❤ ❤ ❤

Question: "How does this work? Why is this one $8,000 and that one $9,200? They look the same to me."

Don't say: "This comes with step-by-step instructions. Why don't we figure it out together?"

Because: This makes you look utterly devoid of expertise about the item, and it directs them to the instructions rather than to the **underlying concept** behind the product. Believe it or not, some people look at the individual parts in order to see the whole, and others look at the whole to understand the parts. The NT is the latter and the SJ the former.

Do Say: "I will be glad to explain it. All of the **systems** we display are designed to make it easier and more efficient to process large amounts of data at a high rate of speed. This particular model — the one you have chosen — evolved out of the idea that none of the others was perfect in and of itself, but when the various features they represent were combined into one machine, even greater productivity could be achieved. Brilliant, isn't it?"

And They May Say: "Well, it is clever. You've made your case. I'll take it."

Because: You have appealed to their love of **innovation**. You have also given them the **context** of the product and, indirectly, acknowledged their **ability** to choose the perfect machine.

NF

Question: "How much are you asking for this?"

Don't Say: "Our prices are set by the manufacturer and we really can't negotiate with customers. Since it's a luxury item, price is not its main feature."

Because: It is **impersonal** and **inflexible**. It also sounds patronizing.

They May Say/Think: "Oh! Well...I guess I won't buy it here."

Because: They will feel they have been snubbed. Nobody likes to feel snubbed.

Try Saying this: "I can see how much you like this, and **I want you to have it**. The manufacturer sets the price, and it's out of our hands, but we're not going to let that stop us, are we? After all, it looks great and your friends will just love it."

So They Can Say: "That's what it's all about, isn't it? I'll take it."

Because: You show interest in their **happiness** — and your own — by settling on a price you can **both feel good** about.

❤ ❤ ❤ ❤ ❤ ❤ ❤ ❤

Question: "I'd like to know your opinion of this compared to the others you've demonstrated for us. Which one do you recommend?"

Don't Say: "It isn't my opinion that matters — it's yours. No one knows your business and its needs as well as you do."

Because: The client is likely to be put off by your refusal to engage on a **person-to-person** level. The client may also **feel isolated** in the decision process, **looking to you** for guidance and getting none.

But if you say this: "**Thank you** for asking — it's unusual for someone to actually ask for my opinion! Seriously, all of these have excellent features, but I think you will **share** my **feeling** that the first one I brought in for you to see will be more easily and effectively used by your **people**, because its so **user- friendly**."

They may say: "Wonderful. Thank you for your help. We will go with the model you have suggested."

Because: You have engaged with them on a **personal** level, you have introduced humor and **reduced** the **tension** of the encounter, you have used language to which the client can **relate**, such as **"feeling"**, **"people"** and **"user-friendly"**. You have taken into account the **impact** of this purchase on the **people** who will be using it.

SP

Question: "I could really use this! What do I have to do to get it?"

Don't Say: "Well, I'll have to sit down with the figures and get back to you with an estimate."

Because: They have told you they want it and they want to take **action** so they can have it — **now**. Asking them to **do nothing but wait** may cause them to be **impatient** and go elsewhere. The response is too **vague** and **passive**. It does not involve any **action** on their part but **waiting**.

But if You Say: "Let me just calculate this now...okay...for $1,625 you can **walk it out the door and be using it in an hour**."

They May Say: "Great! Let's **do** it!"

Because: You have taken **immediate action** so that they can take action now. Don't try to slow them down — they are building their own momentum — go with it.

❤ ❤ ❤ ❤ ❤ ❤ ❤ ❤

Question: "How does it work?"

Don't Say: "It comes with complete **instructions**. I wouldn't even try to guess without **reading them first**!"

Because: That isn't enough information and it defers to the instructions.

Do Say: "Why don't we take it down so you can **try it** for awhile. The parts are made of very sturdy materials, so feel free to **unscrew** the bottom and **take a look**."

They May Say/Think: "Thanks for letting me **take it apart**. I **figured out** what makes it run. I'll take it."

Because: You have allowed them to **handle** and **examine** the item. You have also subtly acknowledged their **ability** to answer their own questions by **interacting** with the item, **hands-on**.

DISCUSSION

In the first question asked by the **SJ**, "Exactly how much does this cost?" We hear a request for information to be given in a **structured** and **precise** manner. The SJ's second question is similar. The SJ views you, the seller, as the authority who will inform him or her of the **requirements** for using and servicing the machinery. It is important to the SJ to **maintain** the product **properly** for **long term** use. We see that the SJ does **not** respond to vague, open-ended responses. The SJ may see them as a runaround.

Now let's look back at the question asked by the **NT**, "What's the price range for this?" Contrary to the SJ, the NT has asked for **general information** about the price and functioning of the item. The NT does **not** respond to details presented in an inflexible manner, and may see this as patronizing. It is important to the NT to see you as the **competent expert**, and him- or herself as **equally knowledgeable** or at least a quick study.

The **NF** asks, "How much are you asking for this?" And "I'd like to know your opinion of this one compared to the others you've demonstrated. Which do you recommend?" Clearly, these questions ask that the information take the form of **dialogue** and **interaction**. The NF responds to a **warm, sincere** seller, a seller who can get **involved personally**. The NF does **not** respond to inflexibility or intellectual sparring. The NF may read this to mean the seller doesn't like them, or it may cause the NF to dislike the seller.

Finally, consider the **SP** who asks, "What do I have to do to get this?" And "How does it work?" The SP asks **direct** questions and wants direct answers. The SP wants to **get involved** with the item itself, **not** necessarily with the seller. Ultimately, the SP will sell him/herself by **handling** the product. The SP does not respond to a sales presentation in which words detach him/her from the product being sold.

While these examples are simple, they have a lot to teach.

First of all, they illustrate the age-old rule of **listening** to the clients and **speaking their language** when responding, even going so far as to repeat back to them some of the words they have used to phrase questions. What these examples also show us is the importance of understanding type and temperament. With this understanding we will be better able to predict what clients value and how we can interact with them most effectively.

Success Builder

1. Describe a situation in which you were unable to communicate effectively with a client or prospect

2. Based on the sample dialogue, what do you thinkcaused the problem in you own example?

3. How could it be handled better next time?

Cases In Point

Now that we understand the four temperaments, let's look at some real-life case studies. One focuses on **NT**s, another on an **NF**, and two focus on **SP**s and **SJ**s.

ROGER AND THE FAMILY BUSINESS

Roger, an **SP**, was an enthusiastic 24-year-old involved in a furniture sales and repair business which had been built by his grandfather and passed on to his father. Roger was excited about the business, and continually tried to spread this excitement to the other employees.

Roger found his biggest obstacle to motivating staff and orienting them to customer service was his own **SJ** father. A seasoned business owner, Roger's father worked in the furniture store since childhood, and belonged to the "old school" of sales.

Roger described it this way: "From dad's point of view, if a customer comes into his store, they want to buy something. If they didn't want to buy something, why come in the store? My dad has no time for price-shoppers or 'difficult' customers. If they stall or hesitate on making the purchase, they're wasting his time, and he has no problem letting them know it! He'll just say 'Listen. I don't know what to tell you! If you want it, you buy it; you don't know what you want, I can't help you.'"

When Roger argued the importance of customer service and professionalism, his father retorted "The same customers been coming in here for 20 years because we got what they want. They don't like it, they can go somewhere else. But they don't. So what's the problem? Business is good." Wow. Talk about taking for granted existing customers! This guy needs to learn never- never number three (taking for granted existing customers)!

In light of his father's attitude, Roger had difficulty changing the attitudes of other employees. After all, they heard their boss talking to customers in a gruff, no-nonsense manner and assumed that must be the way to do it. Roger's concerted efforts to handle customers differently went unnoticed.

Roger had a high hill to climb. His objective was to change the culture of the business, which means its basic beliefs and attitudes toward clients and service. He needed to drag them out of the 1940's and into the 1990's! That much updating required a strategy. As a Sensing-Perceiver (SP), Roger was up to the challenge. His pro-active approach to problem solving would come in handy here.

The first step for Roger was to do some investigative work about the clientele and its needs. Was the clientele stable or changing? Was it made up of longtime repeat customers, new customers, onetime customers or all of the above? What were the reasons these people shopped at this particular store? Because they always had? Because the product was high quality or hard to find elsewhere? Because they received good service there? Because the staff was friendly and made them feel good about purchasing there?

Roger's digging revealed some interesting information. He found that there was a stable base of longtime customers who had shopped at the store for years, but who were getting older and buying less. They did, however, produce a good number of referrals. These customers valued the store's reputation and longevity. There was a small proportion of new repeat customers (coincidentally, Roger found that most of them were his own loyal following). The largest group of customers were onetime buyers who never came back for more service or products. This piece of information about the store's clientele was powerful evidence of the need for change.

The next step was to initiate a serious dialogue with his father, in which Roger would present his discoveries. He knew he would have to use more than his own enthusiasm to win his dad's support. After all, his dad was pretty set in his ways, with definite opinions about how things were to operate in the store.

Fortunately, Roger knew about type. He knew that his father, being a Sensing Judging type (**SJ**), would want to know that changing things would have practical results. And that it would improve the bottom line. Roger knew his dad would keep things as they were unless and until he had concrete evidence to the contrary. So Roger did careful research before approaching his Dad, though he already predicted what the research would show.

Roger delivered a carefully thought-out presentation which emphasized the fact that the largest portion of business came from a steady flow of customers who bought once and never returned. Why didn't they return? Because their needs were somehow not being met. Yes, the selection is great. Yes, the prices are competitive. Yes, the repair work is excellent. No, now that you mention it, the service is not friendly or courteous. The customers who don't care about friendly, courteous service are shrinking in number. The future was not as certain or predictable as it had been before.

Roger's dad saw the point. In fact, he was surprised to hear it. He guessed he wasn't inclined to look at the big picture, what with running the business every day. He became quiet, thinking. Roger relaxed and waited for his father to absorb the implications of what he had just learned.

Recognition of the need for change was the first step toward making the change. It became fairly easy for Roger to rally his father's support, once the reality had sunk in. He solicited his father's commitment to make some changes, and to openly support Roger's efforts with the other employees. He even agreed to set as good an example as possible for the workers who imitated his style.

This done, Roger turned his attention to planning a customer service meeting to be attended by all employees. After this, he would have to monitor progress — especially his dad's — documenting and rewarding effort and success results.

Since Roger, as an **SP**, preferred to charge forward rather than hang back to reflect, he shared the task of documenting improvement with his father, who actually enjoyed it.

KELLY'S CALENDAR

Kelly was a happily employed **SP** selling health club memberships. In many ways, she felt it was the perfect job: fast paced, interesting people, free workouts, kind of glamorous. But in some ways, it really seemed to drag her down: lots of follow-up with prospects and even more paperwork. If only this part of the job could be done by someone else.

For a year, Kelly was able to manage both parts of the job, although she secretly knew she had lost a couple of sales due to lack of follow-up. Kelly was up for a promotion which would involve training new sales staff, more interaction with club members and...more paperwork. Kelly really wanted the promotion and felt she had earned it. Unfortunately, her bosses didn't.

It turned out her "secret" wasn't really a secret. Her supervisor made a habit of tracking prospects, and noticed that Kelly did not have a high rate of converting prospects to members when there was follow-up involved. The supervisor knew Kelly was a dynamo and could close almost anybody who walked in the door. But telephone inquiries were not converting to visits and sales because they were forgotten or set aside.

This was explained to Kelly when she got the news of the lost promotion. Understandably, she was crushed. They told her she needed to be more organized, consistent, and focused on the administrative (SJ) aspect of the job. This left Kelly feeling frustrated because it seemed like yet another job she basically loved was going to end because of the same old things. You see, this scenario was not new to Kelly.

DISCUSSION

Kelly had two things to deal with. First, she kept getting the same feedback from supervisors and managers she worked with. Yet, rather than exploring methods of skill building in the area of organization skills, she would quit her job and move on to something else. The something else always had a lot of appeal, but as she earned more responsibility it had more administrative work. At this point the cycle would begin again. It was beginning to make her feel as though she would never be truly successful at anything.

Kelly needed to gain some self-awareness about the benefits and liabilities of her personality type. She needed to understand that her preferences for Sensing and Perceiving, and her active, energetic style were part of her work habits.

Another part of this was her tendency to focus on the here-and-now, and forget or disregard the past and future until it was too late. Her avoidance of paperwork related to the fact that SP types generally dislike repetitive, routine, tedious tasks. To some, this type of systematic work is calming, relaxing, grounding, satisfying. But not to most SPs.

Kelly did learn about her type and temperament, and she was relieved to learn that she was not alone, and that her work troubles were not due to an inability to work hard and be successful. This new understanding helped her to see that she could be fantastically successful at the health club if she just made a few changes.

The second thing Kelly had to deal with was a lack of organizational skills, which resulted from her lack of interest in organizational tasks. This was where Kelly needed to change some things.

A new calendar and the discipline to use it were all it took to improve Kelly's situation. Two types of information were recorded in this calendar. First, daily appointments and events were entered as they would be in anyone's calendar. Second, "to do" items were entered. These referred to follow-up calls and paperwork deadlines. They were entered this way: whenever

Kelly spoke to a prospect over the phone, she would schedule a visit (rather than suggesting the prospect drop-in unannounced) and enter it into the calendar.

At the same time, pre-visit paperwork was entered in the calendar for two days prior to the visit. At the same time, a note to call and confirm the visit was entered into the calendar for one day prior to the date of the visit. In the event Kelly closed the sale during the visit, the deadline for paperwork relating to that sale was entered into the calendar.

In essence, every task related to a sale was entered at the same time. Kelly would look at her calendar first thing everyday, and see who she was meeting, calling, and closing.

This reduced the possibility of losing things through the cracks when the day got busy. No more surprise visits from prospects she had forgotten she had spoken with. No more lost opportunities, no more lost sales due to lack of organization.

Over a relatively short period of time, Kelly got herself organized, increased her sales, felt better about herself, and eventually got that promotion. Most of all, she had the self- awareness to anticipate the need for organization, rather than realize it after it was too late. She no longer felt incapable of professional success and happiness.

DELORES & JOHN, NT's

Dolores and John, both **NT**s, were free-lance photographers. They were well established professionally, and decided to open up a camera store together, featuring the latest developments (no pun intended!) in photographic equipment. They wanted to have the most knowledgeable staff possible, so they offered a very attractive salary to draw the cream of the crop. In fact, their staff was so competent they required minimal training.

The first few months were somewhat slow, as the store tried to find its niche. There were a handful of "regulars" who came in to talk about their photographic work but rarely bought anything substantial. The "walk-ins" (people coming in off the street with no previous knowledge of the store) never seemed to buy, or to return. The business was floundering.

Meanwhile, the store's leading competitor was going strong (though sellers at Dolores' and John's store looked down their noses, calling it a "hobby store"). It was often bustling with customers — especially on the weekends. Dolores and John visited the store to see what the buzz was all about. As it turned out, everyone there was very friendly, but they certainly didn't seem to have the degree of expertise Dolores and John required of their employees. They were stumped.

DISCUSSION

Dolores and John were extremely knowledgeable and capable when it came to photography. They had a standard of excellence for their store, so they hired people just like them: experts. This was a good idea, in theory. But we all know that product knowledge alone does not make a sale. Sometimes the people who know the most are also the least eloquent or approachable. They don't want to teach us, they want to outsmart us. This is not appealing in a salesperson. This violates three of my never-nevers: treating customers like idiots, trying to impress with jargon, and competing with customers as to who knows more!

The sales team at the competition didn't necessarily have the expertise to answer every imaginable question about photography, but they were friendly and helpful. They were selling to the natural market of amateurs who enjoyed taking good pictures, and they were selling a lot! Dolores and John would have been better off had they hired personable sales professionals who were willing to learn about photography. Better yet, they should have given their original staff of "experts" this book to read!

CHARLES vs. HIS PRODUCT

Outside of work Charles, an NF, described himself as a "people person" who brought out the best in people. He felt in his element when surrounded by friends and family. It was important to Charles to create harmonious relationships, and to connect with people on a personal level. He was thoughtful and spontaneous, enjoying his life and the people in it.

Charles had devoted his professional life to selling financial services to large corporations. Yet, after 20 years in the business, he felt unfulfilled and unhappy. He had difficulty handling the rejections most sales professionals face. He found it increasingly stressful to make his initial approach because of this fear of rejection. Interactions with clients left Charles feeling cold because they were so impersonal. There was no element of helping or relating on a personal level. After 20 years, Charles was still not producing the sales he and his superiors felt he should be. The stress was beginning to sour his enjoyment of life.

DISCUSSION

The disparity between Charles' private and work life created quite a conflict. The conflict was between Charles' personality style and the nature of the product he sold. Financial planning is an impersonal and intangible item. At the corporate level, there is precious little emotion in the sale of a mutual fund. In the language of Typology, financial service is a "Thinking" rather than "Feeling" product because it evokes no emotion and is purchased for nonemotional reasons. Financial services deal in business investments. Executives don't buy high-yield securities to feel proud or special; they buy them to bolster their company financially. The decision to buy is driven by rational analysis of the costs and benefits.

Charles was at odds with his product! No wonder he was unable to gain personal satisfaction in his career. How could he not feel stressed and demoralized? The prospect of continuing in the same field or launching an entirely new career magnified these feelings.

After consideration, it became clear that a better marriage of his **expertise** and **inter-personal** skills would be to sell financial services, not to corporate executives, but to families or retirees. In this arena Charles could engage his clients on the personal level he yearned for, helping them plan their futures. Not only did this fulfill his need to play a helping role, it personalized both his product and his clientele in a way that was meaningful to him. After an extended search, Charles found the position he was looking for. His success was accompanied by a personal transformation that proved, beyond any doubt, the accuracy of his personality type and temperament.

Charles' temperament preferences of i**N**tuitive **F**eeling (**NF**) were engaged as he developed options for his clients so they would be able to rest assured knowing they would be taken care of in the future. And Charles was happy knowing he had helped people. This gave meaning to his work.

❤ ❤ ❤ ❤ ❤ ❤ ❤ ❤

These examples have given you just a glimpse of how temperaments work. In addition, the case of Charles introduces another level of understanding about type that has not been explored before now: the notion that the product itself may be characterized in the language of type. Study of the product suggests methods of selling it. This study includes consideration of who might be drawn to the product and who might never notice it. Who — in terms of professional status — is in a position to make buying decisions? What can we anticipate about their styles before walking in to give a sales presentation?

The inquiry can be revealing. For example, you may find that you have chosen to sell something that truly expresses a part of your personality or represents a value which is important to you. Such a discovery can give new energy to your selling, as well as bring to mind new ideas for product presentation.

Conversely, you may have learned that your type, and that of your product or service, are very different. This may have little impact on how you think and feel about your product. On the other hand, it may be powerfully important. After all, we wouldn't expect a vegetarian to be happy representing a steak wholesaler, or an environmentalist to be happy selling pesticides!

Considering your product's "type" may open your eyes to difficulties you have had in selling the product or relating to the customer. The manner in which the product needs to be sold may be utterly contrary to the way you sell best.

Let's use an example. Retail selling requires the seller to deal with all the people who walk through the door, and to give each of them as much attention as it takes to make a sale. That can get pretty intense on a busy day. If you are an Introvert selling retail, chances are you feel drained at the end of the day — or at the end of any given interaction. You surely would have realized this about yourself, and now you know why you feel that way. As an Introvert, your energy comes from turning inward for reflection and space. Being bombarded with demands from the external world means that there is often little opportunity to reflect and re-energize.

Now ask yourself this question: "I have considered the type of my product. There is a target clientele which is most likely to want my product. What is the type of that clientele?" The answer to this question will tell you a lot about how you relate to your customers.

❤ ❤ ❤ ❤ ❤ ❤ ❤ ❤

What follows are responses to interview questions I asked of professional sellers. While many people were interviewed, the quotes I have selected capture the essence of the four temperaments as they relate to sales.

When asked what they like most about their work in sales, this is how the temperaments responded:

SJ Stockbroker: I am not inherently interested in stocks and bonds. I work to support my family and to allow us to enjoy family traditions such as skiing in the winter and beach trips every summer.

SP Stockbroker: I love my work when it's fast-paced, but it isn't, always. The market goes through cycles. When it gets boring, I just take a couple of weeks off!

NF Fund-raiser: I tend to light up and get excited by the product I'm promoting. Someone once said to me, "You were so into it, I felt I'd miss something if I didn't buy a subscription!"

NT Real Estate Broker: I am very competitive, and I like to be the best at what I do. I participate in regional and national sales contests within the field, because I generally enjoy my work most when there's a prize at stake. Each potential sale is a challenge, and the feeling I get when I've closed a deal is like a real victory.

SP Real Estate Broker: My favorite part of this work is the actual signing of the contract. Not because the deal is finished but because, at that point, things move very fast and its very exciting. It could be midnight when the papers are ready; everyone's nervous and I'm in charge, and I run all over town all night getting signatures. Sometimes I don't get home til 3 am — I love it!

NF Merchandise Wholesaler: What keeps me in sales is the energy I get from interacting with people about something I really believe in.

NT Retailer: Retail is exciting because with every new customer who walks through the door, there's an opportunity to use a new approach to selling the product. I get very creative. I think that eventually I will develop the most effective approach to almost any given sales situation!

SJ Automobile Dealer: This a family business. People trust the continuity and stability that represents; they know we're not going anywhere, so they can trust buying their cars here.

❤ ❤ ❤ ❤ ❤ ❤ ❤ ❤

On the other hand . . . Here are some responses to the question "What do you like least about your work in sales?":

NF Bookseller: I can't do this on a full-time basis because I get too wired from all the customers. It's like I'm too tuned-in to them. If one is in a bad mood, I pick up on it and feel tense. It's hard to detach myself.

SP Sales Manager for a Manufacturing Wholesaler: I get really tired of all the bureaucratic red tape that goes into a corporate client's decision to purchase. It's so obvious to me that my equipment is what the company needs and wants, and yet they make the decision so difficult.

NT Electronics Sales: I get impatient with clients who don't make smart decisions. When they decide not to purchase my system, it's one thing. But when their reasoning is totally illogical, I become frustrated and I guess it shows.

SJ Life Insurance: I find it hard to understand people who don't plan. They live for the moment, without looking ahead to when their kids will need money for college, or to when they're ready to retire. By then it will be too late.

SP Computer Hardware: My sales team is required to go through periodic training on assembly, use and service of the computers we sell. It seems like such a waste of time. I think it should be part of the job to learn it yourself so you can sell it. But most people just wait around for the training programs, then they moan about having to go. If they would just take the time to figure it out for themselves, maybe the company could phase out the training requirement.

SJ Art Dealer: I don't particularly like working on commission. It's stressful, not knowing exactly how much money I will be taking home at the end of the pay period. It makes it really hard to plan. When I bought this business I took everyone off of commission and put them on salary or hourly wages plus bonus. It's less stressful for everyone.

NT Antiques Dealer: I've been in this business for 40 years because it is so fascinating. Every new piece that comes into my store has a story behind it — history behind it — and I learn new things each day. I confess that the actual sales aspect of the business is tedious for me. It takes me away from my exploration, and it annoys me when customers are more interested in getting a good deal than in their new piece of history.

NF Telemarketer: It isn't easy having people respond angrily or just hang up the phone while I'm talking. I try to start out with something humorous. Once in a while it pays off and I speak to someone who is friendly and interested; I wish it were more often!

♥ ♥ ♥ ♥ ♥ ♥ ♥ ♥

The awareness of type helps alleviate some of these feelings. However, it only goes so far. A good manager ultimately realizes that his/her staff needs to be deployed effectively — each to his/her own maximized talents and minimized weaknesses.

The exceptional manager reading this book sees the possibilities. Bringing this approach to a sales staff not only helps the individuals tap into the best they have to offer — it shows them how to utilize each other's strengths to make more sales.

♥ ♥ ♥ ♥ ♥ ♥ ♥ ♥

TEMPERAMENTAL ADVICE

NT
- Try to put aside your need for competency; get out of your own head and let the client set the tone. Guide the customer in a non-threatening manner. Don't intimidate clients with too much information and jargon.

NF
- Try not to take every lost sale personally — it doesn't mean the client didn't like you or that you are not good at selling. Learn what you can from lost sales and then let go of them.

SJ
- Try to stay away from "shoulds" with clients. Let them decide what is best for them. Don't lose your cool if your close goes off course or is delayed. Go with the flow!

SP
- Try to stay focused and to keep the client focused. Be careful not to rush the decision. Be patient with clients who ask a lot of questions, even if you know they aren't pertinent.

Success Builder

1. What type or temperament issues prevent you from being the best seller you could be?

2. Brainstorm strategies for resolving those issues.

3. If your product or service had a four-letter type or two-letter temperament, what would it be?

4. How does this compare with the way you see yourself?

5. What do you like best about sales? Least?

Team Selling

Quality and communication are being emphasized in business, government and the military as part of the Total Quality Management movement. TQM is also linked to the concept of team work. Organizations of all kinds are investing time and resources in training staff to work as teams rather than as competitors. For example, General Electric awards team bonuses to some divisions as a way of stimulating team effort.

The theory of personality types, called Typology, has direct applications to team building because it increases awareness and appreciation of our own styles, as well as the work styles of our colleagues. It helps us to cultivate and use everyone's natural strengths.

The more people there are involved in any given project, the more likely there is to be diversity of type within the group. Diversity of styles produces its own variety, which can be expressed positively as flexibility. A group of people, some of whom are **Sensing**, some of whom are **iNtuitive**, some of whom are **Thinking** types, and some of whom are **Feeling** types, is more likely to consider all options because it is not limited to one point of view. Often, a team working together on a project will be homogeneous because of the nature of the project. For example, in hi-tech computer sales, there will more likely be Sensors who don't realize how they could benefit from the input of iNtuitive types. While Sensors may be drawn to sell this product because of its hands-on complexity, iNtuitives may be the marketing geniuses who develop ways of bringing the product to the public, based on it's benefits and visual appeal.

It is important to understand that personal differences which may be frustrating can be put to good use if we learn to value them properly.

Salespeople historically have worked independently because, as we know, they must compete intensely for business. Unless people in different regions are working together to address different markets, a company sales "team" barely resembles a team in any traditional sense. It can be back-stabbing and cut-throat, as each member competes for his or her own advantage.

While this may keep people on their toes, ultimately it generates negative energy. It promotes counter-productive interactions between people. Trust cannot be established among coworkers. This affects the quality of life in the workplace. It creates stress, paranoia, and ineffectiveness because less effort is placed on the **quality** of customer service. The emphasis is, instead, placed on the **quantity** of "conquests", in the form of sales or new clients.

The crucial concept we must each embrace is that **quality creates quantity**. Customers won't buy a second time if they weren't satisfied the first time. They won't buy at all if they don't like the manner of the staff, or if they can't get the information they need. For example, allowing a prospect to wait on the showroom floor until you finish your telephone conversation will usually not result in a sale. Quality **does** di-rectly contribute to the bottom line, and requires serious consideration.

Introducing the notions of type and typological differences to the sales setting is the best way to mold individual sellers into a team. Suddenly we begin to look upon each other as a resource, each with something to contribute to overall productivity. The willingness to learn from each other replaces previous avoidance and competition. A cooperative environment replaces the stressful, secretive environment in which we must protect and defend our little piece of the action; an effort that takes so much energy from us individually and as a group. Our individual and collective energy is freed-up to provide optimal customer service.

Remember the story of Roger and his dad? Their problem was an out-moded attitude toward customers which was demonstrated by dad and adopted throughout the staff. Roger brought everyone together to explore a new approach based on top-notch customer service. The result was a happier and more effective sales team.

When teaming with another seller, the ideal match-up is with someone of opposite type, or at least a couple of preferences opposite yours. That allows the two of you to compliment each other and truly approach the sale from a position of strength. It allows you to cover the bases, so to speak, in terms of presenting the product in the language and style most comfortable to the customer. A team with one i**N**tuitive and one **S**ensor will be able to provide the customer with the necessary facts and details **as well as** the possibilities of the product. It may become clear at some point that the customer is getting what they need from one or the other of you, then it is time for a turnover.

The issues of teamwork and turnover sales go hand in hand. Imagine what could be accomplished by restructuring the sales setting based on these two concepts. Instead of losing a sale due to lack of rapport with a client, the client could, without penalty to the original salesperson, be turned-over to someone else who might be better able to close the sale. The opener and the closer both benefit, and there is built-in incentive to repeat the practice of turnovers when the sale might otherwise be lost altogether.

This method can reduce competitiveness and backstabbing because it simply does not pay to work that way. Let me give an example. If I am determined to make a sale independently, and if I fail to make that sale, I have just lost money out of my bonus. If, on the other hand, I realize at some point during the sale that there is a poor connection between the client and myself, or if there is something ineffective about the way we communicate with each other, I would be wise to turn it over to someone who might have better luck.

Success Builder

1. How is teamwork being used in your organization?

2. How could it be better utilized?

3. Who would be a good match-up with you, from a type and temperament perspective?

Turnover Sales

I remember an experience in which I was team selling and the customer—I don't recall whether it was a woman or a man—directed all questions and eye contact to my partner. Initially I felt insulted. I wanted to say, "Hey!, I'm here too...can't you see me standing right in front of you?!?." But my knowledge of personality styles helped to close the sale. The objectivity of my **Thinking** preference helped me to recognize that a rapport was being established by my partner. I let go of my need to be acknowledged by the client. I gracefully withdrew from the action, allowing my partner to continue with his progress.

It can be tough on the ego to turnover a sale because we don't have the knowledge or information required by the client. But we must do it so that the sale will be made and the client will be served.

I have also had the experience in which I was team selling, and the client seemed to express a clear preference for my style, rather than my partner's. If this client only had the option of dealing with my partner, she probably would have declined the purchase out of discomfort with his style. By approaching the client together, we gave her an alternative to leaving empty-handed and unsatisfied.

There is an art to turning over a sale and working as a team. There is a point at which the client sets the terms and defines your role. At this point you must identify that role and stay in it. The object is not to be right or to have the last word. You can be right as rain and broker than broke. The object is to satisfy the customer and establish a lasting relationship.

When turning over a sale to another seller, you must truly turn it over. That is: GET OUT. Don't hang around trying to stay involved. If you are going to turn the sale over, you must stop talking and walk away, period. What you're doing by turning over a sale is deferring to the expertise of another salesperson. In other words, you're establishing their credibility with the customer. The proper way to turn over a sale is not to say, "Well, I obviously am not able to make this sale. Maybe someone else will be able to deal with you, because I sure can't!" The proper way is to establish the other seller's credibility by saying something to this effect: "Your questions are all valid and, unfortunately, I don't have the knowledge to help you make an informed decision. But Josephine, over here, does have expertise in this area. She will be able to help you better than I can, with this." Having said that, introduce Josephine and excuse yourself. If you linger, trying to contribute so as not to appear ignorant, you are completely discrediting Josephine and yourself.

You've heard the expression, "Never let them see you sweat". When it comes to turnovers, never let them see your hunger for the sale. Its a turn off.

Success Builder

1. What awareness did you gain about yourself and others from this chapter?

2. How will you change your use of turnovers as a result?

Snapshots of Sellers

Now that we understand the basic principles of the personality preferences — Extraversion/Introversion (**E/I**), Sensing/iNtuition (**S/N**), Thinking/Feeling (**T/F**), and Judging/Perceiving (**J/P**) — let's explore how they work in real world settings.

The next section contains one page devoted to each of the sixteen personality types. These pages list **opportunities** that may result from each preference (indicated by a + symbol), as well as **obstacles** presented by each preference (indicated by a - symbol). Of course every characteristic will not apply to each person, so use the snapshots as a basic guidelines for improving your performance. Remember: we all possess the eight preferences and can benefit from their strengths. Find the page that best describes you. Read it. Read it again. And again. Become aware of how your preferences reinforce your interactions, as well as the obstacles they often present. Whenever you encounter one of these opportunities and obstacles, write it down and learn from it. Generate some options for handling the situation better next time. Look to the other personality styles for ideas.

Once you have integrated the information about your own personality style, you will learn to identify your effective areas and the areas you need to improve when dealing with others.

ESTJ

E + Focuses energy outward, engaging the client
+ Easily establishes rapport via light banter/shmoozing
+ Seeks potential customers on and off the job

E - May talk too much, filling silences
- May overwhelm buyer with too much information
- May be redundant in the sales presentation

S + Often masters details of the product/thorough knowledge
+ Provides specific, clear answers to questions
+ Realistic view of things

S - May not readily generate options or be creative about selling
- May not readily anticipate client needs, or future needs for product
- May focus too much on detail, losing sight of the customer's needs

T + Comfortable with the bottom-line dollars and cents element of sales
+ Orients client to objective, logical reasons to buy
+ Values quality

T - May undervalue the emotional appeal of a product, focusing on the "bottom line"
- May appear disinterested or arrogant to the customer
- May value being right over making the sale

J + Good at follow-up & tracking sales
+ Organized
+ Good at keeping focus & reaching closure

J - May be too oriented to closing the sale, and appear pushy
- May be impatient with slow decision-makers
- May be inclined to tell customers what to do and why

ISTJ

I + Good at listening
+ Able to summarize customer's needs
+ Articulates in a few, well-chosen phrases

I - May be too quiet and provide too little information
- May internalize the interaction v. fully participating with client
- May not communicate/externalize energy for product being sold

S + Often masters details of the product/thorough knowledge
+ Provides specific, clear answers to questions
+ Realistic view of things

S - May not readily generate options or be creative about selling
- May not readily anticipate client needs, or future needs for product
- May focus too much on detail, losing sight of the customer's needs

T + Comfortable with the bottom-line dollars and cents element of sales
+ Orients client to objective, logical reasons to buy
+ Values quality

T + May undervalue the emotional appeal of a product, focusing on the "bottom line"
- May appear disinterested or arrogant to the customer
- May value being right over making the sale

J + Good at follow-up & tracking sales
+ Organized
+ Good at keeping focus & reaching closure

J - May be too oriented to closing the sale, and appear pushy
- May be impatient with slow decision-makers
- May be inclined to tell customers what to do and why

ENTJ

E + Focuses energy outward, engaging the client
+ Easily establishes rapport via light banter/shmoozing
+ Seeks potential customers on and off the job

E - May talk too much, filling silences
- May overwhelm buyer with too much information
- May be redundant in the sales presentation

N + Good at generating options and seeing possibilities
+ Able to put purchase in larger perspective
+ Able to communicate enthusiasm for the product

N - May generate too many options and lose sight of the client's focus
- May disdain details and technical aspects of the product
- May exaggerate or misrepresent product inadvertently, due to level of enthusiasm

T + Comfortable with the bottom-line dollars and cents element of sales
+ Orients client to objective, logical reasons to buy
+ Values quality

T - May undervalue the emotional appeal of a product, focusing on the "bottom line"
- May appear disinterested or arrogant to the customer
- May value being right over making the sale

J + Good at follow-up & tracking sales
+ Organized
+ Good at keeping focus & reaching closure

J - May be too oriented to closing the sale, and appear pushy
- May be impatient with slow decision-makers
- May be inclined to tell customers what to do and why

INTJ
· · · · · · · · · · ·

I + Good at listening
+ Able to summarize customer's needs
+ Articulates in a few, well-chosen phrases

I - May be too quiet and provide too little information
- May internalize the interaction v. fully participating with client
- May not communicate/externalize energy for product being sold

N + Good at generating options and seeing possibilities
+ Able to put purchase in larger perspective
+ Able to communicate enthusiasm for the product

N - May generate too many options and lose sight of the client's focus
- May disdain details and technical aspects of the product
- May exaggerate or misrepresent product inadvertently, due to level of enthusiasm

T + Comfortable with the bottom-line dollars and cents element of sales
+ Orients client to objective, logical reasons to buy
+ Values quality

T - May undervalue the emotional appeal of a product, focusing on the "bottom line"
- May appear disinterested or arrogant to the customer
- May value being right over making the sale

J + Good at follow-up & tracking sales
+ Organized
+ Good at keeping focus & reaching closure

J - May be too oriented to closing the sale, and appear pushy
- May be impatient with slow decision-makers
- May be inclined to tell customers what to do and why

ESFJ

E + Focuses energy outward, engaging the client
+ Easily establishes rapport via light banter/shmoozing
+ Seeks potential customers on and off the job

E - May talk too much, filling silences
- May overwhelm buyer with too much information
- May be redundant in the sales presentation

S + Often masters details of the product/thorough knowledge
+ Provides specific, clear answers to questions
+ Realistic view of things

S - May not readily generate options or be creative about selling
- May not readily anticipate client needs, or future needs for product
- May focus too much on detail, losing sight of the customer's needs

F + Good at cultivating loyal customers
+ Good at adding a personal touch to the buying experience
+ Values what's best for customer

F - May avoid conflict over price (haggling)
- May take lost sales personally
- May not be bottom-line oriented enough to generate profits

J + Good at follow-up & tracking sales
+ Organized
+ Good at keeping focus & reaching closure

J - May be too oriented to closing the sale, and appear pushy
- May be impatient with slow decision-makers
- May be inclined to tell customers what to do and why

ISFJ

I + Good at listening
+ Able to summarize customer's needs
+ Articulates in a few, well-chosen phrases

I - May be too quiet and provide too little information
- May internalize the interaction v. fully participating with client
- May not communicate/externalize energy for product being sold

S + Often masters details of the product/thorough knowledge
+ Provides specific, clear answers to questions
+ Realistic view of things

S - May not readily generate options or be creative about selling
- May not readily anticipate client needs, or future needs for product
- May focus too much on detail, losing sight of the customer's needs

F + Good at cultivating loyal customers
+ Good at adding a personal touch to the buying experience
+ Values what's best for customer

F - May avoid conflict over price (haggling)
- May take lost sales personally
- May not be bottom-line oriented enough to generate profits

J + Good at follow-up & tracking sales
+ Organized
+ Good at keeping focus & reaching closure

J - May be too oriented to closing the sale, and appear pushy
- May be impatient with slow decision-makers
- May be inclined to tell customers what to do and why

ENFJ

E + Focuses energy outward, engaging the client
+ Easily establishes rapport via light banter/shmoozing
+ Seeks potential customers on and off the job

E - May talk too much, filling silences
- May overwhelm buyer with too much information
- May be redundant in the sales presentation

N + Good at generating options and seeing possibilities
+ Able to put purchase in larger perspective
+ Able to communicate enthusiasm for the product

N - May generate too many options and lose sight of the client's focus
- May disdain details and technical aspects of the product
- May exaggerate or misrepresent product inadvertently, due to level of enthusiasm

F + Good at cultivating loyal customers
+ Good at adding a personal touch to the buying experience
+ Values what's best for customer

F - May avoid conflict over price (haggling)
- May take lost sales personally
- May not be bottom-line oriented enough to generate profits

J + Good at follow-up & tracking sales
+ Organized
+ Good at keeping focus & reaching closure

J - May be too oriented to closing the sale, and appear pushy
- May be impatient with slow decision-makers
- May be inclined to tell customers what to do and why

INFJ

··········

I + Good at listening

+ Able to summarize customer's needs

+ Articulates in a few, well-chosen phrases

I - May be too quiet and provide too little information

- May internalize the interaction v. fully participating with client

- May not communicate/externalize energy for product being sold

N + Good at generating options and seeing possibilities

+ Able to put purchase in larger perspective

+ Able to communicate enthusiasm for the product

N - May generate too many options and lose sight of the client's focus

- May disdain details and technical aspects of the product

- May exaggerate or misrepresent product inadvertently, due to level of enthusiasm

F + Good at cultivating loyal customers

+ Good at adding a personal touch to the buying experience

+ Values what's best for customer

F - May avoid conflict over price (haggling)

- May take lost sales personally

- May not be bottom-line oriented enough to generate profits

J + Good at follow-up & tracking sales

+ Organized

+ Good at keeping focus & reaching closure

J - May be too oriented to closing the sale, and appear pushy

- May be impatient with slow decision-makers

- May be inclined to tell customers what to do and why

ESTP

E   +   Focuses energy outward, engaging the client

     +   Easily establishes rapport via light banter/shmoozing

     +   Seeks potential customers on and off the job

E   -   May talk too much, filling silences

     -   May overwhelm buyer with too much information

     -   May be redundant in the sales presentation

S   +   Often masters details of the product/thorough knowledge

     +   Provides specific, clear answers to questions

     +   Realistic view of things

S   -   May not readily generate options or be creative about selling

     -   May not readily anticipate client needs, or future needs for product

     -   May focus too much on detail, losing sight of the customer's needs

T   +   Comfortable with the bottom-line dollars and cents element of sales

     +   Orients client to objective, logical reasons to buy

     +   Values quality

T   -   May undervalue the emotional appeal of a product, focusing on the "bottom line"

     -   May appear disinterested or arrogant to the customer

     -   May value being right over making the sale

P   +   Comfortable dealing with unpredictable events

     +   Able to give customer flexibility in decision-making process

     +   Able to guide the customer to "Yes" through exploratory questioning

P   -   May not be closure-oriented enough to complete sales

     -   May not be thorough in follow-up efforts

     -   May not see the need for timeliness

ISTP

I + Good at listening
+ Able to summarize customer's needs
+ Articulates in a few, well-chosen phrases

I - May be too quiet and provide too little information
- May internalize the interaction v. fully participating with client
- May not communicate/externalize energy for product being sold

S + Often masters details of the product/thorough knowledge
+ Provides specific, clear answers to questions
+ Realistic view of things

S - May not readily generate options or be creative about selling
- May not readily anticipate client needs, or future needs for product
- May focus too much on detail, losing sight of the customer's needs

T + Comfortable with the bottom-line dollars and cents element of sales
+ Orients client to objective, logical reasons to buy
+ Values quality

T - May undervalue the emotional appeal of a product, focusing on the "bottom line"
- May appear disinterested or arrogant to the customer
- May value being right over making the sale

P + Comfortable dealing with unpredictable events
+ Able to give customer flexibility in decision-making process
+ Able to guide the customer to "Yes" through exploratory questioning

P - May not be closure-oriented enough to complete sales
- May not be thorough in follow-up efforts
- May not see the need for timeliness

ENTP

E + Focuses energy outward, engaging the client

+ Easily establishes rapport via light banter/shmoozing

+ Seeks potential customers on and off the job

E - May talk too much, filling silences

- May overwhelm buyer with too much information

- May be redundant in the sales presentation

N + Good at generating options and seeing possibilities

+ Able to put purchase in larger perspective

+ Able to communicate enthusiasm for the product

N - May generate too many options and lose sight of the client's focus

- May disdain details and technical aspects of the product

- May exaggerate or misrepresent product inadvertently, due to level of enthusiasm

T + Comfortable with the bottom-line dollars and cents element of sales

+ Orients client to objective, logical reasons to buy

+ Values quality

T - May undervalue the emotional appeal of a product, focusing on the "bottom line"

- May appear disinterested or arrogant to the customer

- May value being right over making the sale

P + Comfortable dealing with unpredictable events

+ Able to give customer flexibility in decision-making process

+ Able to guide the customer to "Yes" through exploratory questioning

P - May not be closure-oriented enough to complete sales

- May not be thorough in follow-up efforts

- May not see the need for timeliness

INTP

I + Good at listening
+ Able to summarize customer's needs
+ Articulates in a few, well-chosen phrases

I - May be too quiet and provide too little information
- May internalize the interaction v. fully participating with client
- May not communicate/externalize energy for product being sold

N + Good at generating options and seeing possibilities
+ Able to put purchase in larger perspective
+ Able to communicate enthusiasm for the product

N - May generate too many options and lose sight of the client's focus
- May disdain details and technical aspects of the product
- May exaggerate or misrepresent product inadvertently, due to level of enthusiasm

T + Comfortable with the bottom-line dollars and cents element of sales
+ Orients client to objective, logical reasons to buy
+ Values quality

T - May undervalue the emotional appeal of a product, focusing on the "bottom line"
- May appear disinterested or arrogant to the customer
- May value being right over making the sale

P + Comfortable dealing with unpredictable events
+ Able to give customer flexibility in decision-making process
+ Able to guide the customer to "Yes" through exploratory questioning

P - May not be closure-oriented enough to complete sales
- May not be thorough in follow-up efforts
- May not see the need for timeliness

ESFP

E + Focuses energy outward, engaging the client
+ Easily establishes rapport via light banter/shmoozing
+ Seeks potential customers on and off the job

E - May talk too much, filling silences
- May overwhelm buyer with too much information
- May be redundant in the sales presentation

S + Often masters details of the product/thorough knowledge
+ Provides specific, clear answers to questions
+ Realistic view of things

S - May not readily generate options or be creative about selling
- May not readily anticipate client needs, or future needs for product
- May focus too much on detail, losing sight of the customer's needs

F + Good at cultivating loyal customers
+ Good at adding a personal touch to the buying experience
+ Values what's best for customer

F - May avoid conflict over price (haggling)
- May take lost sales personally
- May not be bottom-line oriented enough to generate profits

P + Comfortable dealing with unpredictable events
+ Able to give customer flexibility in decision-making process
+ Able to guide the customer to "Yes" through exploratory questioning

P - May not be closure-oriented enough to complete sales
- May not be thorough in follow-up efforts
- May not see the need for timeliness

ISFP
. . . .

I + Good at listening

+ Able to summarize customer's needs

+ Articulates in a few, well-chosen phrases

I - May be too quiet and provide too little information

- May internalize the interaction v. fully participating with client

- May not communicate/externalize energy for product being sold

S + Often masters details of the product/thorough knowledge

+ Provides specific, clear answers to questions

+ Realistic view of things

S - May not readily generate options or be creative about selling

- May not readily anticipate client needs, or future needs for product

- May focus too much on detail, losing sight of the customer's needs

F + Good at cultivating loyal customers

+ Good at adding a personal touch to the buying experience

+ Value's what's best for customer

F - May avoid conflict over price (haggling)

- May take lost sales personally

- May not be bottom-line oriented enough to generate profits

P + Comfortable dealing with unpredictable events

+ Able to give customer flexibility in decision-making process

+ Able to guide the customer to "Yes" through exploratory questioning

P - May not be closure-oriented enough to complete sales

- May not be thorough in follow-up efforts

- May not see the need for timeliness

ENFP

E + Focuses energy outward, engaging client
+ Easily establishes rapport via light banter/shmoozing
+ Seeks potential customers on and off the job

E - May talk too much, filling silences
- May overwhelm buyer with too much information
- May be redundant in the sales presentation

N + Good at generating options and seeing possibilities
+ Able to put purchase in larger perspective
+ Able to communicate enthusiasm for the product

N - May generate too many options and lose sight of the client's focus
- May disdain details and technical aspects of the product
- May exaggerate or misrepresent product inadvertently, due to level of enthusiasm

F + Good at cultivating loyal customers
+ Good at adding a personal touch to the buying experience
+ Values what's best for customer

F - May avoid conflict over price (haggling)
- May take lost sales personally
- May not be bottom-line oriented enough to generate profits

P + Comfortable dealing with unpredictable events
+ Able to give customer flexibility in decision-making process
+ Able to guide the customer to "Yes" through exploratory questioning

P - May not be closure-oriented enough to complete sales
- May not be thorough in follow-up efforts
- May not see the need for timeliness

INFP

I + Good at listening
   + Able to summarize customer's needs
   + Articulates in a few, well-chosen phrases

I - May be too quiet and provide too little information
   - May internalize the interaction v. fully participating with client
   - May not communicate/externalize energy for product being sold

N + Good at generating options and seeing possibilities
   + Able to put purchase in larger perspective
   + Able to communicate enthusiasm for the product

N - May generate too many options and lose sight of the client's focus
   - May disdain details and technical aspects of the product
   - May exaggerate or misrepresent product inadvertently, due to level of enthusiasm

F + Good at cultivating loyal customers
   + Good at adding a personal touch to the buying experience
   + Values what's best for customer

F - May avoid conflict over price (haggling)
   - May take lost sales personally
   - May not be bottom-line oriented enough to generate profits

P + Comfortable dealing with unpredictable events
   + Able to give customer flexibility in decision-making process
   + Able to guide the customer to "Yes" through exploratory questioning

P - May not be closure-oriented enough to complete sales
   - May not be thorough in follow-up efforts
   - May not see the need for timeliness

Snapshots of Buyers

ESTJ
· · · · · · · · · ·

E
- is approachable and conversational
- keeps the conversation going when there are lulls
- shares personal information not directly related to the business at hand
- talks through the decision-making process

S
- asks for specific information
- emphasizes the practical aspects of the product
- takes the things you say quite literally
- shops for something they will use in the near future

T
- appears skeptical at first, not easily won-over by your charm
- is oriented to the bottom line, not necessarily to establishing rapport with you
- asks you for information more than for opinions
- bases the decision to buy or not to buy on logical analysis of the costs and benefits

J
- is straight-forward about what they like and dislike
- shops with a purpose, and in advance
- asks deliberate questions which they may read from a list they have brought with them
- has little or no trouble making the decision to buy or not to buy

ISTJ
. . . .

I • looks quietly rather than approaching you
   • speaks relatively little, letting you do most of the talking
   • appears to think to him - or herself about the purchase
   • does not readily catch the contagion of your passion for the product

S • asks for specific information
   • emphasizes the practical aspects of the product
   • takes the things you say quite literally
   • shops for something they will use in the near future

T • appears skeptical at first, not easily won-over by your charm
   • is oriented to the bottom line, not necessarily to establishing rapport with you
   • asks you for information more than for opinions
   • bases the decision to buy or not to buy on logical analysis of the costs and benefits

J • is straight-forward about what they like and dislike
   • shops with a purpose, and in advance
   • asks deliberate questions which they may read from a list they have brought with them
   • has little or no trouble making the decision to buy or not to buy

ENTJ
. . . .

E • is approachable and conversational
  • keeps the conversation going when there are lulls
  • shares personal information not directly related to the business at hand
  • talks through the decision-making process

N • asks general questions
  • appears to "tune out" when you get into the details of the product
  • does not focus on one thing for too long, before becoming interested in something else
  • is most intrigued by what is interesting about the product

T • appears skeptical at first, not easily won-over by your charm
  • is oriented to the bottom line, not necessarily to establishing rapport with you
  • asks you for information more than for opinions
  • bases the decision to buy or not to buy on logical analysis of the costs and benefits

J • is straight-forward about what they like and dislike
  • shops with a purpose, and in advance
  • asks deliberate questions which they may read from a list they have brought with them
  • has little or no trouble making the decision to buy or not to buy

INTJ

· · · · · · · · · ·

I · looks quietly rather than approaching you
  · speaks relatively little, letting you do most of the talking
  · appears to think to him- or herself about the purchase
  · does not readily catch the contagion of your passion for the product

N · asks general questions
  · appears to "tune out" when you get into the details of the product
  · does not focus on one thing for too long, before becoming interested in something else
  · is most intrigued by what is interesting about the product

T · appears skeptical at first, not easily won-over by your charm
  · is oriented to the bottom line, not necessarily to establishing rapport with you
  · asks you for information more than for opinions
  · bases the decision to buy or not to buy on logical analysis of the costs and benefits

J · is straight-forward about what they like and dislike
  · shops with a purpose, and in advance
  · asks deliberate questions which they may read from a list they have brought with them
  · has little or no trouble making the decision to buy or not to buy

ESFJ

E • is approachable and conversational
   • keeps the conversation going when there are lulls
   • shares personal information not directly related to the business at hand
   • talks through the decision-making process

S • asks for specific information
   • emphasizes the practical aspects of the product
   • takes the things you say quite literally
   • shops for something they will use in the near future

F • wants to interact with you in a friendly way
   • is interested in your opinions about the product
   • seems embarrassed about asking for a lower price
   • bases the decision to buy or not to buy on their "gut" feeling or other subjective means

J • is straight-forward about what they like and dislike
   • shops with a purpose, and in advance
   • asks deliberate questions which they may read from a list they have brought with them
   • has little or no trouble making the decision to buy or not to buy

ISFJ

I
- looks quietly rather than approaching you
- speaks relatively little, letting you do most of the talking
- appears to think to him - or herself about the purchase
- does not readily catch the contagion of your passion for the product

S
- asks for specific information
- emphasizes the practical aspects of the product
- takes the things you say quite literally
- shops for something they will use in the near future

F
- wants to interact with you in a friendly way
- is interested in your opinions about the product
- seems embarrassed about asking for a lower price
- bases the decision to buy or not to buy on their "gut" feeling or other subjective means

J
- is straight-forward about what they like and dislike
- shops with a purpose, and in advance
- asks deliberate questions which they may read from a list they have brought with them
- has little or no trouble making the decision to buy or not to buy

ENFJ

....

E • is approachable and conversational
  • keeps the conversation going when there are lulls
  • shares personal information not directly related to the business at hand
  • talks through the decision-making process

N • asks general questions
  • appears to "tune out" when you get into the details of the product
  • does not focus on one thing for too long, before becoming interested in something else
  • is most intrigued by what is interesting about the product

F • wants to interact with you in a friendly way
  • is interested in your opinions about the product
  • seems embarrassed about asking for a lower price
  • bases the decision to buy or not to buy on their "gut" feeling or other subjective means

J • is straight-forward about what they like and dislike
  • shops with a purpose, and in advance
  • asks deliberate questions which they may read from a list they have brought with them
  • has little or no trouble making the decision to buy or not to buy

INFJ

I
- looks quietly rather than approaching you
- speaks relatively little, letting you do most of the talking
- appears to think to him- or herself about the purchase
- does not readily catch the contagion of your passion for the product

N
- asks general questions
- appears to "tune out" when you get into the details of the product
- does not focus on one thing for too long, before becoming interested in something else
- is most intrigued by what is interesting about the product

F
- wants to interact with you in a friendly way
- is interested in your opinions about the product
- seems embarrassed about asking for a lower price
- bases the decision to buy or not to buy on their "gut" feeling or other subjective means

J
- is straight-forward about what they like and dislike
- shops with a purpose, and in advance
- asks deliberate questions which they may read from a list they have brought with them
- has little or no trouble making the decision to buy or not to buy

ESTP

E • is approachable and conversational
  • keeps the conversation going when there are lulls
  • shares personal information not directly related to the business at hand
  • talks through the decision-making process

S • asks for specific information
  • emphasizes the practical aspects of the product
  • takes the things you say quite literally
  • shops for something they will use in the near future

T • appears skeptical at first, not easily won- over by your charm
  • is oriented to the bottom line, not necessarily to establishing rapport with you
  • asks you for information more than for opinions
  • bases the decision to buy or not to buy on logical analysis of the costs and benefits

P • seems to enjoy browsing, with no particular focus
  • shops at the last minute
  • is open to suggestions
  • has difficulty deciding whether or not to buy, and what

ISTP

. . . .

I • looks quietly rather than approaching you
   • speaks relatively little, letting you do most of the talking
   • appears to think to him- or herself about the purchase
   • does not readily catch the contagion of your passion for the product

S • asks for specific information
   • emphasizes the practical aspects of the product
   • takes the things you say quite literally
   • shops for something they will use in the near future

T • appears skeptical at first, not easily won- over by your charm
   • is oriented to the bottom line, not necessarily to establishing rapport with you
   • asks you for information more than for opinions
   • bases the decision to buy or not to buy on logical analysis of the costs and benefits

P • seems to enjoy browsing, with no particular focus
   • shops at the last minute
   • is open to suggestions
   • has difficulty deciding whether or not to buy, and what

ENTP
. . . .

E • is approachable and conversational
- keeps the conversation going when there are lulls
- shares personal information not directly related to the business at hand
- talks through the decision-making process

N • asks general questions
- appears to "tune out" when you get into the details of the product
- does not focus on one thing for too long, before becoming interested in something else
- is most intrigued by what is interesting about the product

T • appears skeptical at first, not easily won- over by your charm
- is oriented to the bottom line, not necessarily to establishing rapport with you
- asks you for information more than for opinions
- bases the decision to buy or not to buy on logical analysis of the costs and benefits

P • seems to enjoy browsing, with no particular focus
- shops at the last minute
- is open to suggestions
- has difficulty deciding whether or not to buy, and what

INTP

I
- looks quietly rather than approaching you
- speaks relatively little, letting you do most of the talking
- appears to think to him- or herself about the purchase
- does not readily catch the contagion of your passion for the product

N
- asks general questions
- appears to "tune out" when you get into the details of the product
- does not focus on one thing for too long, before becoming interested in something else
- is most intrigued by what is interesting about the product

T
- appears skeptical at first, not easily won-over by your charm
- is oriented to the bottom line, not necessarily to establishing rapport with you
- asks you for information more than for opinions
- bases the decision to buy or not to buy on logical analysis of the costs and benefits

P
- seems to enjoy browsing, with no particular focus
- shops at the last minute
- is open to suggestions
- has difficulty deciding whether or not to buy, and what

ESFP

E • is approachable and conversational
  • keeps the conversation going when there are lulls
  • shares personal information not directly related to the business at hand
  • talks through the decision-making process

S • asks for specific information
  • emphasizes the practical aspects of the product
  • takes the things you say quite literally
  • shops for something they will use in the near future

F • wants to interact with you in a friendly way
  • is interested in your opinions about the product
  • seems embarrassed about asking for a lower price
  • bases the decision to buy or not to buy on their "gut" feeling or other subjective means

P • seems to enjoy browsing, with no particular focus
  • shops at the last minute
  • is open to suggestions
  • has difficulty deciding whether or not to buy, and what

ISFP

I
- looks quietly rather than approaching you
- speaks relatively little, letting you do most of the talking
- appears to think to him- or herself about the purchase
- does not readily catch the contagion of your passion for the product

S
- asks for specific information
- emphasizes the practical aspects of the product
- takes the things you say quite literally
- shops for something they will use in the near future

F
- wants to interact with you in a friendly way
- is interested in your opinions about the product
- seems embarrassed about asking for a lower price
- bases the decision to buy or not to buy on their "gut" feeling or other subjective means

P
- seems to enjoy browsing, with no particular focus
- shops at the last minute
- is open to suggestions
- has difficulty deciding whether or not to buy, and what

ENFP
. . . .

E • is approachable and conversational
  • keeps the conversation going when there are lulls
  • shares personal information not directly related to the business at hand
  • talks through the decision-making process

N • asks general questions
  • appears to "tune out" when you get into the details of the product
  • does not focus on one thing for too long, before becoming interested in something else
  • is most intrigued by what is interesting about the product

F • wants to interact with you in a friendly way
  • is interested in your opinions about the product
  • seems embarrassed about asking for a lower price
  • bases the decision to buy or not to buy on their "gut" feeling or other subjective means

P • seems to enjoy browsing, with no particular focus
  • shops at the last minute
  • is open to suggestions
  • has difficulty deciding whether or not to buy, and what

INFP

I • looks quietly rather than approaching you
• speaks relatively little, letting you do most of the talking
• appears to think to him- or herself about the purchase
• does not readily catch the contagion of your passion for the product

N • asks general questions
• appears to "tune out" when you get into the details of the product
• does not focus on one thing for too long, before becoming interested in something else
• is most intrigued by what is interesting about the product

F • wants to interact with you in a friendly way
• is interested in your opinions about the product
• seems embarrassed about asking for a lower price
• bases the decision to buy or not to buy on their "gut" feeling or other subjective means

P • seems to enjoy browsing, with no particular focus
• shops at the last minute
• is open to suggestions
• has difficulty deciding whether or not to buy, and what

Putting It All Together

Typology offers you a method for turning sale-breaking errors into sale-making opportunities. By continually examining your interactions with prospects and customers, and honing your skills with people whose styles are different from yours, you can reach a level of effectiveness that exceeds your highest ambition.

Take time to think about how you **Approach, Observe, Assess, and Act**. Visualize this with a typical customer, if you can imagine one, or compare it to an atypical customer. Be aware of your style as you interact with prospects. When is it effective and when less effective? This type of self-reflection will keep you moving toward success.

Again, your rate of improvement depends upon the degree to which you focus on others as well as yourself. Read the personal type description in the section entitled "Snapshots." Read the others. After working with a prospect or customer, see what helpful clues lie in the descriptions of customer types. With a little effort, you will improve your interactions with coworkers as well.

And don't forget about your product. The better you understand all its facets and the ways in which it can appeal to different people, the more you will sell. Practice presenting your product to different customer types. An examination of the product from other points of view is a powerful way of anticipating objections and overcoming them.

Temperaments are a quicker, easier way around types. The strategies in the temperaments chapter were designed to bring temperaments to life through dialogue. There are suggestions for breaking out of the limits of your own style and communicating more effectively with customers of all types. In addition, the "Live Cases" provide more real-life examples of temperaments. Return to these sections as you begin to recognize the impact of temperament styles in your work as a sales pro. And the advice at the end of the chapter — one or two pointers for each temperament - caution us against handcuffing ourselves with negative habits.

Here are some suggestions for using temperaments with customers. First, you must practice identifying temperament styles in the people around you. It's important to practice so sales won't be lost while you're getting the hang of it. Use any or all of these tips, regardless of your own temperament style (sometimes experimenting outside of our comfort zone can bring exciting results!).

SUGGESTION #1: The SJ Approach.

Structure the information from this book in your own way so that you will have clear and specific guidelines to work from. After all, my way of structuring this material reflects my way of perceiving and judging; it can't possibly work for everyone. Structure can make ideas more concrete.

SUGGESTION #2: The NT Approach

Observe, study and experiment with the temperament styles you encounter until you feel comfortable with the behavioral distinctions. Learning from observation brings theory to life so it can be used with confidence - and competence.

SUGGESTION #3: The NF Approach.

Practice with friends and coworkers. Use the ideas in this book to achieve better communication with customers and more satisfaction in sales. This is a very people-friendly method to understanding differences between people. Therefore, engage others in practicing with you.

SUGGESTION #4: *The SP Approach.*

Make this into a game for yourself and those you work with. The concepts and strategies can be used in a playful way if you don't want to use it with customers. In your observations of other people selling, guess at the type and temperament dynamics between them and their customers.

Remember our four rules about interacting with customers? Let's take a moment to revisit them.

THE NEVER-NEVERS

1. Never make people feel inferior
2. Never try to impress with jargon
3. Never take existing customers for granted
4. Never compete with the customer

Never again hold yourself back by telling yourself "I can't deal with customers like him/her. They're too...." Put these strategies to work and you'll deal better with all types of people. You will have more awareness of your own blind spots and biases. And you will be more receptive to customers who require a different approach.

Instead of writing off these individuals, view them as a challenge. The challenge is for you to use the skills and information in this book to be more effective with **all** customers.

We've covered a lot of ground in these pages, and laid the foundation for a new approach to sales. The methods and strategies are simple but require practice. The result will likely be more sales, larger sales, repeat business, increased enjoyment and a stronger sense of meaning in your work.

So carry this little guide with you, take lots of notes, practice identifying styles, and watch your sales skyrocket. You are now prepared to close sales and win the customer's heart!

❤ ❤ ❤ ❤ ❤ ❤ ❤ ❤

notes

notes

notes

About the author...

Emily King Parker has been writing and presenting on the topic of personality type and sales for the last eight years. Her company, King Street Associates, has assisted many organizations in reaching their sales goals by using the techniques described in this book. Some clients have included: Mellon Bank, PNC Bank, PriceCostco, IBM and British Aerospace.

Currently Ms. Parker consults for a leading technology firm in the Washington, D.C. area.